The Mystery of the Moving Hand

The story of Belshazzar and Daniel,
Daniel 5 for children

Written by Larry Burgdorf

Illustrated by Ed Koehler

CONCORDIA PUBLISHING HOUSE · SAINT LOUIS

Belshazzar was a foolish king.
He thought that he ruled everything.
He really knew, but didn't care,
That one true God ruled everywhere.

The gods he worshiped were all fake—
Just statues that someone would make.
They couldn't speak and couldn't hear;
Just metal, wood, and stone, it's clear.

One day, Belshazzar gave a feast.
A thousand people came, at least.
They ate and drank quite heartily
And joined the king's idolatry.

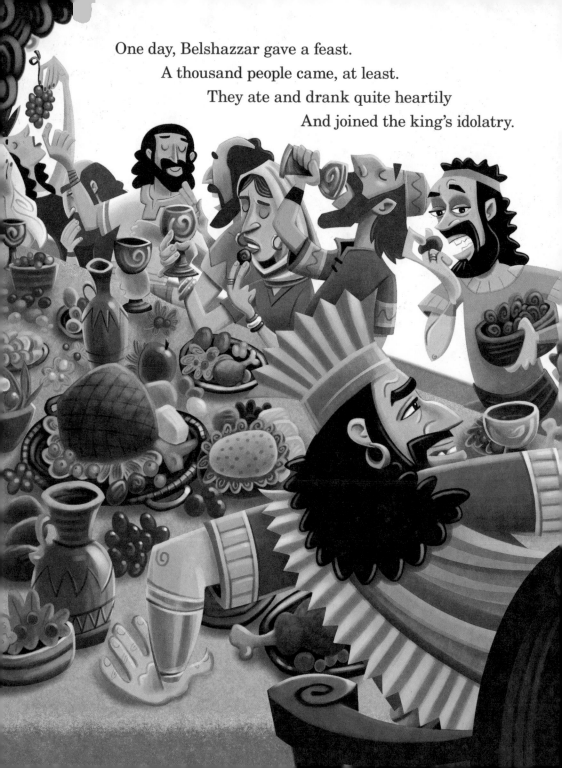

Belshazzar knew, for he'd been told,
That these fake gods—some wood, some gold—
Were dead as doornails through and through,
But there was one God
        who is true.

Belshazzar didn't care a bit.
What he did next compounded it.
He sent his slaves to bring to them
The vessels from Jerusalem.

These cups of silver and of gold
Were sacred things, and very old.
Their purpose was to glorify
The one true God, who reigns on high.

But now Belshazzar used them for
His rowdy feast, and what is more,
They raised those cups to praise their fakes,
Those poor, dumb idols—goodness sakes!

mene mene

What happened then is truly weird—
A disconnected hand appeared!
And quickly, everybody froze!
Knees knocked together; heartbeats rose!

The hand wrote words upon the wall,
Which simply terrified them all.
"Mene, Mene," wrote the hand,
But no one there could understand.

It wrote some more, which gave them fits
And scared the king out of his wits.
Their question was, "What does this mean;
These strange new words that we have seen?"

The frightened king gave a command
To all the wise men in the land.
"Come, read the words upon the wall
And tell their meaning to us all."

The wise men came, but soon they knew
They didn't have a single clue.
Just then, the queen came in the room
And tried to cheer their
heavy gloom.

She told the king, "There is a man
Who can do what nobody can.
His name is Daniel, and I know
He'll read the words that scare you so."

Daniel responded to the call
And came into the banquet hall.
He stepped inside and looked about,
Then gave the king a bawling out.

He said, "I'll read the words, O king,
But first I'll say another thing.
You do not do what you should do
And God is going to punish you.

You knew the God that you should praise
But chose instead that idol craze.
The 'Mene, Mene' means that you
Have badly failed. King you are through."

The lesson from this is that you
Can praise the one God
who is true!

That same God sent a Savior, who
Has opened heav'n for me and you.

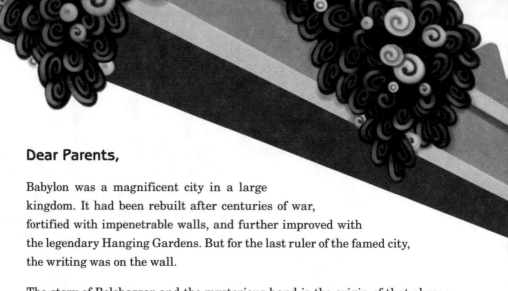

Dear Parents,

Babylon was a magnificent city in a large kingdom. It had been rebuilt after centuries of war, fortified with impenetrable walls, and further improved with the legendary Hanging Gardens. But for the last ruler of the famed city, the writing was on the wall.

The story of Belshazzar and the mysterious hand is the origin of that phrase. Belshazzar, a descendant of King Nebuchadnezzar, inherited his power and wealth. An arrogant and inexperienced ruler, Belshazzar felt invincible, and so he celebrated.

Belshazzar gave an extravagant feast. At least a thousand guests were treated to great quantities of food and drink. They worshiped the many gods of Babylon—the sun god, the moon god, and others. And then, Belshazzar toasted the heathen gods, using the sacred vessels that had been stolen from Solomon's temple. In so doing, Belshazzar publicly mocked the one true God.

The words on the wall were enough to get Belshazzar's attention. Daniel interpreted them as a dire warning. That night, the city fell to the invading Persian army and Belshazzar was killed.

What does this story mean for us? We are guilty of distracting ourselves with gods of our own making—false gods. We forget that God is the source of all that is good; we ignore or even defy Him. But God in His mercy gave us His Word in the Bible, so we may know Him and His plan for our salvation through Christ.

The Editor